LENTEN
Survival
Guide
FOR KIDS

WHATEVER HAPPENS,
DON'T LOSE THIS BOOK
BEFORE
ASH WEDNESDAY.

LENTEN Survival Guide FOR KIDS

by PETER CELANO

I'M SUPPOSED TO DO WHAT?!

PARACLETE PRESS
BREWSTER, MASSACHUSETTS

2015 Second Printing
2014 First Printing

Lenten Survival Guide for Kids: I'm Supposed to Do What?!

Copyright © 2014 by Paraclete Press, Inc.

ISBN: 978-1-61261-521-9

Most quotations from Holy Scripture (yes, there are quite a few, but don't let that scare you away!) are taken from the New Revised Standard Version, copyright © 1989 by the Division of Christian Education of the National Council of Churches of Christ in the U.S.A. Used by permission. All rights reserved.

Other Bible quotations marked "The Message" are taken from *The Message: Catholic/ Ecumenical Edition*. Copyright © 1993, 1994, 1995, 1996, 2000, 2001, 2002, 2013. Used by permission of NavPress Publishing Group. Used by permission.

The Paraclete Press name and logo (dove on cross) is a trademark of Paraclete Press, Inc.

Library of Congress Cataloging-in-Publication Data
Celano, Peter.
  Lenten survival guide for kids : I'm supposed to do what?! / Peter Celano.
    pages cm
  ISBN 978-1-61261-521-9
  1. Lent—Juvenile literature. 2. Spiritual life—Catholic Church--Juvenile literature.
  3. Catholic Church—Doctrines—Juvenile literature. I. Title.
  BV85.C45 2014
  263'.92—dc23   2014000153

10 9 8 7 6 5 4 3 2

Published by Paraclete Press
Brewster, Massachusetts
www.paracletepress.com
Printed in the United States of America

This book is dedicated
to faithful followers of
Lent everywhere.

Contents

What's the Purpose of Lent?

You may have heard about this thing called Lent. This is your guide to not only surviving it, but also— dare we suggest?—loving it. Wait. Allow us to explain . . .

There are no ghouls, vampires, and ghosts in Lent. Whoever told you there were, never listen to what they say ever again.

Lent is a season of the year, a time that comes around on the calendar a little while after the Christmas decorations are taken down. It can be a bit frightening how quickly the days of "Joy to the World" and "Away in a Manger" turn to giving up stuff we love . . . hearing words like "repentance" . . . and ideas such as *fasting*. More on fasting later.

In your imagination, Lent is most of all probably the time of year when your mother or father starts to talk about how everyone has to give something up. Something you really, really like—you have to steer clear of during Lent.

Now, keep in mind that many kids smarter than you have tried to be clever about this in the past. For example, you may have already thought of this one: giving up something that you'd be happy to give up just about anytime. It's an old trick. The conversation goes something like this:

You: I have thought and prayed about what to give up for Lent, Mom. [Pausing to place your hand over your heart, or to look quickly up toward heaven.] Here's what I've decided—I think I'll give up making my bed and taking out the trash. How's that?

Mom: I see. Okay, in that case, I will give up giving you an allowance.

You: Um. Never mind.

Why do we do Lent every year anyway? Sure, it comes around on the calendar, but why do it?

Why—for instance—would anyone willingly give up something that seems so good throughout the rest of the year? Who does that help?

Who are we kidding—Lent *is* a bit frightening. That is, if you take it seriously, it can be frightening. And since you are reading this book, we are going to assume that you're willing to take it seriously.

But, in addition to giving things up, this is also the time of year when your pastor may start talking about getting more serious about prayer, about dedication to God, about going to confession, about reading the Bible, about identifying sin in your life, and about doing more good for others. So to answer the question, *what's the point?* The point is: getting serious.

There are other baffling words as well. What in the world, for instance, is "penitence" all about? Stay tuned.

The common denominator in all of this is what? Seriousness. So tell us, have you gotten serious? Are you ready?

What Lent Is

★ Okay, this is what Lent is. Nitty gritty stuff.

ON THE CALENDAR ⋯⋗

Lent begins on Ash Wednesday and lasts for either thirty-eight or forty days, depending on how you count them. (Everybody always excludes Sundays during Lent, because Sundays are "feast days," or times of celebration, all year round, since it was on a Sunday that Christ rose from the dead.) In the Roman Catholic Church, Lent continues until Holy Thursday, ending that evening. So for Catholics, you count thirty-eight days starting with Ash Wednesday. In most other churches that observe Lent, you count forty days and the final day of Lent is Holy Saturday, the very last day before Easter.

So no matter who you are, Lent will carry you through the approximately six weeks just before Easter.

There can be no Easter without Lent.

And Easter Sunday makes no sense without Ash Wednesday, those thirty-eight to forty days of Lent, Holy Thursday, Good Friday, and Holy Saturday.

So settle in. Get ready to fully participate in these important days ahead.

For the next few years, this is when Ash Wednesday falls on the calendar. Make a note of it. This is when Lent begins.

2014: Wednesday, March 5

2015: Wednesday, February 18

2016: Wednesday, February 10

2017: Wednesday, March 1

Then, mark every weekday and Saturday until at least Holy Thursday. Those are the days of prayer and discipline for anyone intending to observe the season of Lent. And unless we're mistaken, that's you!

ABOUT ASH WEDNESDAY

Ash Wednesday is the day when many Christians go to church to have ashes put on their foreheads in the shape of a cross. That alone makes it pretty unusual! Why do this? Because Ash Wednesday is the first day of Lent, and we begin with this stark reminder of our mortality, which means simply that every human being will someday die. When you understand that fact clearly, the importance of being "right" with God begins to feel much more urgent!

Ash Wednesday reminds us that we will someday meet God face-to-face.

On Ash Wednesday, your pastor will say to you, while placing ashes on your forehead, "You started out as dirt, you'll end up dirt" (Genesis 3:19, *The Message*), or perhaps: "Repent, and believe in the good news" (Mark 1:15).

When you leave church with ashes on your forehead, what will you do? Everyone will see them there. They may even stare. Will you wipe them off before walking outside, or before heading to school? That's up to you. But keep this in mind: every Christian is supposed to be a witness for God in the world. Ash Wednesday could be a good day for that.

ABOUT HOLY THURSDAY ····⋮

Holy Thursday is the thirty-eighth day of Lent. By this day, your Lenten journey will have (hopefully!) taught you many things. And in church, you will again find that the service is out of the ordinary. This is the day on which we remember the Last Supper—when Jesus dined with his disciples on the night before his arrest. This is also the day when we remember how Jesus washed the feet of his disciples, one-by-one, even Judas, who Jesus knew was about to betray him!

You may even see your pastor, or deacon, washing people's feet in your church on Holy Thursday. Don't worry if that idea (and the sight of it) makes you uncomfortable at first. We think that's probably the point Jesus was making that first time: it can feel uncomfortable to care for another person so closely as to wash their dirty, stinky feet—and it's okay to feel that way. Jesus did it for a reason. He did everything for a reason!

There is another word that's often associated with this day: *maundy*. It's not a word you will encounter in any other context, ever. But Holy Thursday is sometimes also called "Maundy Thursday."

Chances are good that you probably don't know Latin; your grandparents or great-grandparents probably knew Latin. Kids everywhere used to learn

Latin in grade school, and they would have known that *maundy* is a word that comes from a Latin word, *mandatum*, and means "commandment." Why *commandment*? Because after Jesus washed the feet of the disciples, he said to them: "Let me give you a new command: Love one another. In the same way I loved you, you love one another. This is how everyone will recognize that you are my disciples—when they see the love you have for each other." (John 13:34–35, *The Message*)

ABOUT GOOD FRIDAY

Good Friday is . . . You probably already know what Good Friday is, right? Well, let's just be sure.

There are three days on the calendar every year that are the most important days in the life of a Christian. They are:

1) Christmas. We know that you know about that one, right? Christ was born.

2) Easter. Surely Easter is emblazoned on your memory, too. Christ is risen. The tomb was empty!

3) And then there's **Good Friday**.

The first Good Friday took place two days before the first Easter. It was on Good Friday that Jesus was tortured, crucified, and died. So . . . you're probably wondering, what's so good about a day like that?!

Well, Easter wouldn't make much sense without Good Friday, now would it? Jesus had to die in order to rise again. And Jesus died for you.

THE BIBLE AND LENT

If you are one of the smart ones, you may object to Lent by saying that it is not mentioned anywhere in the Bible. If you did say that, you'd actually be right.

The word *Lent* never appears in Holy Scripture. But neither does "Christmas" or "Easter," so settle down. What we do during Lent is still inspired by a few important passages from the Bible, such as Nehemiah 9:1–2, Esther 4:1, 3, and Daniel 9:3–4. Here they are, in order.

RESPONDING TO SIN WITH PENITENCE

Everyone sins, and sometimes we respond by admitting our sin and doing what we now call "penitence." Nehemiah 9:1-2 says:

"Now on the twenty-fourth day of this month the people of Israel were assembled with fasting and in sackcloth, and with earth on their heads. Then those of Israelite descent separated themselves from all foreigners, and stood and confessed their sins."

What the Israelites did is similar to what we do, today, when we fast or pray more at certain times of year like Lent, asking forgiveness for our sins. They were penitent all together, as a community event!

Why should we talk to God more at this time of year? Someone could just as easily say: Why don't you *always* pray to God? Well, that really is the ultimate goal, but praying at least during Lent is a good start.

RESPONDING TO EVIL WITH MOURNING

When King Ahasuerus (don't worry about pronouncing it correctly—hardly anyone ever does) of Persia, a kingdom that stretched from India all the way to Ethiopia, issued a decree that all of the Jews were to be killed, a Jewish man named Mordecai publicly mourned for his people. The book of Esther 4:1, 3 says:

> "When Mordecai learned all that had been done, Mordecai tore his clothes and put on sackcloth and ashes, and went through the city, wailing with a loud and bitter cry. . . . In every province, wherever the king's command and his decree came, there was great mourning among the Jews, with fasting and weeping and lamenting."

Does this make any sense to us today? What good does it do to tear your clothes when someone is mean to you or someone else? Not much—at least it probably won't mean much to the mean people. But showing that sort of mourning in an outward action was a way of appealing to God for safety and protection.

WAITING UPON THE LORD ⋯⋮

There once was a smart, sensitive young man—probably still in his teenage years—named Daniel. He was famous among his people as someone who could understand the meaning of dreams and even predict future events. One day Daniel read about a prophecy that said Jerusalem and all of its inhabitants were in serious danger. He wanted to do something, but he didn't know what to do—so he prayed. The book of Daniel 9:3–4 says:

"Then I turned to the Lord God, to seek an answer by prayer and supplication with fasting and sackcloth and ashes. I prayed to the LORD my God and made confession."

There's that sackcloth and ashes again! And supplication—what in the world is *supplication* anyway?

The point is: Daniel prayed, and he prayed seriously. These were not the quick bop prayers that we sometimes offer up, but real "sweat on the forehead" prayers. As you will discover, Lent is about *that* kind of praying.

Don't worry: we don't do actual sackcloth and ashes anymore. So keep shampooing your hair in the shower. Keep washing your hands every day. There are no brownie points for filthy faces that look sad.

However, Christians everywhere know that there are lessons to be learned from the ways that the Israelites of the Old Testament showed their hearts to God. They often demonstrated how they felt, and the passion they desired for faith, in outward ways—like "sackcloth and ashes."

We don't do that anymore. But we *do* need to have hearts that are desperately seeking to be closer to God, and hearts that are sincerely sad about what we've done that is selfish, or mean, or insincere. That is, again, where prayer—the serious kind of prayer—comes in. Especially during Lent.

Then, there is the most important passage of all in the Bible for seeing how Lent came to be: the story of Jesus fasting in the wilderness. Here is how it happened:

FASTING FOR FORTY DAYS LIKE JESUS DID ┅┅❖

After Jesus was baptized in the Jordan River by John the Baptist, he "was led by the Spirit into the wilderness," three of the Gospels tell us. He went into the Judean Desert. Don't worry about exactly where that is—it is in the Holy Land—and a lot hotter than it is in Ohio or California. The Gospel says that he went there "to be tempted by the devil."

In other words, God the Father wanted Jesus the Son to face real temptation—the sort of temptation that human beings are likely to face. But Jesus faced his temptations in a way that is unlike what we normally do. The book of Matthew, chapter 4, verse 2 says:

"He fasted forty days and forty nights, and afterwards he was famished."

You may want to read the whole passage about this event in the life of Jesus. If you do, look at Matthew 4:1–11. You will see that Jesus didn't eat for forty days (or he ate very little—fasting often means eating little rather than eating nothing) so that he could pray and think and listen for what God wanted him to do with his life.

What Lent Definitely Is Not

Where do we start, exactly? There is so much to say about what Lent is not. People easily become confused on this subject. In fact, we're glad you are reading this book, because we want to set you, at least, straight. You can then please set others straight.

As you've already read, Lent is not about "giving up" silly things. It is not about making sad faces to show how difficult life has suddenly become for you. (Need we start explaining how most of the world would think that giving up candy bars or soda for forty days sounds just plain silly? According to the Bread for the World website, 925 million people around the world go hungry each day. That's about three times as many people as live in the United States going to bed every night with pain in their bellies from lack of nutrition. So please don't talk about the *terrible hardship* you are undergoing by giving up M&Ms and Coca-Cola for a few weeks.)

Lent is, in fact, not about giving things up, period. Yes, you should give something up, or *lots* of things, depending on who you are and how you currently live. But it doesn't have to be *things*.

People also give up certain habits, or behaviors, during Lent, but that is also not really the point. Consider it this way: people do not stop smoking just because everyone else around them seems to be quitting. No—a person stops smoking because they don't want smoke-breath, they don't want to develop lung disease or cancer, and they want to live to a healthy old age!

So instead of focusing on what you may give up, take some time to consider why you are giving it up. You give stuff up for Lent because you want to pay more attention to God and others than yourself. You are testing yourself—and allowing God to test you—to see if, by giving up something that maybe you are too focused on in everyday life, you can concentrate more on him during these forty days.

OTHER CRAZY IDEAS OUT THERE ABOUT LENT

We know that you have seen movies. You have seen television shows. You have read books and heard stories about crazy things that people once did, maybe sometimes still do, to their bodies when they are trying to "get serious" about God. Well, that's not Lent either.

Beating up your body is never what God wants. Nowhere in the Bible does God tell us to hurt ourselves. Jesus said, "Blessed are those who are persecuted for righteousness' sake, for theirs is the kingdom of heaven" (Matthew 5:10). He didn't say, "Blessed are those who pummel themselves for righteousness' sake. . . ."

But then, there is this thing called "fasting." We mentioned it briefly before and promised that we'd come back to it.

It's a funny word, *fasting*. It sounds like someone who is really quick on his feet, rather than someone who abstains from food. The verb *fast* means "to hold fast," or "standing firm," even though you may be eating less, or nothing at all, for a while.

You'll find fasting all over the Bible. Moses fasted before he received the Ten Commandments from God on Mount Sinai (see Deuteronomy 9:7–21). David fasted to show his humility before God (see Psalm 35:13), and to repent for a serious sin (2 Samuel 12:15–25). The apostle Paul fasted for three days after he saw God like a blinding light on the road to Damascus, in order to wait and see and listen for what he should do next (see Acts 9:9).

Fasting is not beating up your body. First Peter 3:14 says, "even if you do suffer for doing what is right, you are blessed." Trust us, you aren't suffering when you eat well most of the time and then fast every now and then. It may feel like suffering, but it isn't. Instead, you are simply remembering what it feels like to be hungry.

Now, here's the trick. When you feel a little bit hungry, rather than quickly going to the kitchen and filling your stomach, go to your Bible or to your knees, and ask God to fill your hunger. Then, commit yourself to doing more of God's work in the world. What can you do today to represent Jesus in your neighborhood?

You can eat something later.

40 Days of Survival Tactics

1.

···> REMEMBER,
DON'T JUST GIVE SOMETHING UP.

Wear a string around your wrist if you have to, but somehow, make sure that you remember that whenever you are craving the thing you gave up, you are supposed to turn your mind toward God instead.

Why not pray? Not in some big look-at-me sort of way, like, "Oh my, I would LOVE to eat a Hershey's bar right now, but I can't!" No. Pray quietly, to yourself.

Then, pray quietly for people who are in the greatest need. You may never have met such people, but they are people just like you, and just like us. We are talking about the people that Jesus talked about as those in the greatest need of help—those who Jesus compared to himself. In Matthew chapter 25, Jesus told this story about what the end of life might look like:

All the nations will be gathered before him,
and he will separate people one from another
as a shepherd separates the sheep from the
goats, and he will put the sheep at his right
hand and the goats at the left. Then the king
will say to those at his right hand, "Come,
you that are blessed by my Father, inherit
the kingdom prepared for you from the
foundation of the world; for I was hungry and
you gave me food, I was thirsty and you gave
me something to drink, I was a stranger and
you welcomed me, I was naked and you gave
me clothing, I was sick and you took care of
me, I was in prison and you visited me."

MATTHEW 25:32–36

2.

PRAY THE WORDS OF THE BIBLE.

Here are two important, complete Psalms that will help you. The phrases and verses that appear in **bold** are perhaps the best parts—and you could even memorize those!

Psalm 51

Have mercy on me, O God,
   according to your steadfast love;
according to your abundant mercy
   blot out my transgressions.
Wash me thoroughly from my iniquity,
   and cleanse me from my sin.

For I know my transgressions,
   and my sin is ever before me.
Against you, you alone, have I sinned,
   and done what is evil in your sight,
so that you are justified in your sentence
   and blameless when you pass judgment.
Indeed, I was born guilty,
   a sinner when my mother conceived me.

You desire truth in the inward being;

   therefore teach me wisdom in my secret heart.

Purge me with hyssop, and I shall be clean;

   wash me, and I shall be whiter than snow.

Let me hear joy and gladness;

   let the bones that you have crushed rejoice.

Hide your face from my sins,

   and blot out all my iniquities.

Create in me a clean heart, O God,

   and put a new and right spirit within me.

Do not cast me away from your presence,

   and do not take your holy spirit from me.

Restore to me the joy of your salvation,

   and sustain in me a willing spirit.

Then I will teach transgressors your ways,
and sinners will return to you.
Deliver me from bloodshed, O God,
O God of my salvation,
and my tongue will sing aloud of your
deliverance.

O Lord, open my lips,
and my mouth will declare your praise.
For you have no delight in sacrifice;
if I were to give a burnt-offering, you would
not be pleased.
The sacrifice acceptable to God is a broken spirit;
a broken and contrite heart, O God, you will
not despise.

Do good to Zion in your good pleasure;
  rebuild the walls of Jerusalem,
then you will delight in right sacrifices,
  in burnt-offerings and whole burnt-offerings;
  then bulls will be offered on your altar.

Consider sharing these bold verses with a friend or a family member who you think might need some spiritual support. These are great promises:

Psalm 91

You who live in the shelter of the Most High,
  who abide in the shadow of the Almighty,
will say to the Lord, **"My refuge and my fortress;
  my God, in whom I trust."**

For he will deliver you from the snare of the fowler
    and from the deadly pestilence;
he will cover you with his pinions,
    and **under his wings you will find refuge;**
    his faithfulness is a shield and buckler.
You will not fear the terror of the night,
    or the arrow that flies by day,
or the pestilence that stalks in darkness,
    or the destruction that wastes at noonday.
A thousand may fall at your side,
    ten thousand at your right hand,
    but it will not come near you.
You will only look with your eyes
    and see the punishment of the wicked.

Because you have made the Lord your refuge,
    the Most High your dwelling-place,
no evil shall befall you,
    no scourge come near your tent.

For **he will command his angels concerning you
to guard you in all your ways.**
On their hands they will bear you up,
  so that you will not dash your foot against a
  stone.
You will tread on the lion and the adder,
  the young lion and the serpent you will
trample under foot.
Those who love me, I will deliver;
  I will protect those who know my name.
When they call to me, I will answer them;
  I will be with them in trouble,
  I will rescue them and honor them.
With long life I will satisfy them,
  and show them my salvation.

3. GET TO KNOW THE STATIONS OF THE CROSS.

Do you know about the stations of the cross? You should. There are fourteen of them, and they may even be present in your church, even if you never noticed them there before. Usually they are sculpture or paintings hanging on the walls of the nave.

There is no time of the year better to pray your way through the "stations" (that's the shorthand way of referring to them). Take some time during Lent to get to know them. As you do, you will encounter two additional and important phrases for understanding what Lent is all about. These are phrases that haven't come up in this book yet, until now: "The Passion of Our Lord" and "Holy Week."

The stations of the cross depict the most important moments in the Passion of Our Lord—what we call the events of his arrest, trial, and crucifixion, the most important events of Holy Week, which is the final week in the life of Christ that we remember every year. Sometimes we use shorthand to call the Passion of Our Lord simply "Christ's Passion."

Here are the fourteen traditional stations. See if you can find them in your church. Stand before them, one at a time, and pray with gratitude for what Christ did for you long ago. (If you don't find them in your church, look them up online. You'll find plenty of images depicting these events. You can pray through the stations just as easily at home.)

One small detail: this list of the stations is the most recent one, approved by Pope John Paul II on Good Friday in 1991. All of these fourteen stations are mentioned specifically in the Gospels. There is an older, traditional list of stations that you will find in many churches that is somewhat different. Of course, all of them are good, but this list of fourteen is probably the best since they are all straight from Holy Scripture:

The Stations of the Cross

Jesus prays in the Garden of Gethsemane.

Jesus is betrayed by Judas.

Jesus is condemned by the Sanhedrin.

Peter denies Jesus three times.

Pilate judges Jesus.

They scourge Jesus and crown him with thorns.

Jesus takes up his cross.

Simon helps Jesus carry the cross.

Jesus meets the women of Jerusalem.

They crucify Jesus.

Jesus promises his kingdom to a repentant thief.

Jesus asks Mary and John to care for each other.

Jesus dies on the cross.

They lay Jesus in the tomb.

The Stations of the Cross— with Bible verses

Jesus prays in the Garden of Gethsemane.

Matthew 26:36–41

Jesus is betrayed by Judas.

Mark 14:43–46

Jesus is condemned by the Sanhedrin.

Luke 22:66–71

Peter denies Jesus three times.

Matthew 26:69–75

Pilate judges Jesus.

Mark 15:1–5, 15

They scourge Jesus and crown him with thorns.

John 19:1–3

Jesus takes up his cross.
John 19:6, 15–17

Simon helps Jesus carry the cross.
Mark 15:21

Jesus meets the women of Jerusalem.
Luke 23:27–31

They crucify Jesus.
Luke 23:33–34

Jesus promises his kingdom to a repentant thief.
Luke 23:39–43

Jesus asks Mary and John to care for each other.
John 19:25–27

Jesus dies on the cross.
Luke 23:44–46

They lay Jesus in the tomb.
Matthew 27:57–60

Above all, remember: there would have been no Easter without Good Friday. It is important to be with Christ in his Passion before we can really understand the meaning of his Resurrection.

A Few Prayers and Practices —Only for Kids

Okay, if you haven't heard this loudly and clearly already by this point, Lent is a time to pray. Pray. Pray every day in Lent, and when it starts to feel boring, or too repetitive, find new ways to pray, be creative! But don't stop praying.

No one can ever explain how good, blessed things happen to people who pray.

PRAYERS FOR WHEN YOU ARE ALONE

A Prayer for the Week before Lent

Dear God, please show me what I should give up
this year for Lent.
I will listen.
And when I've given up what you suggested,
and I'm missing it,
Remind me to pray to you.
Remind me to thank you for everything.
I love you.
I'm listening.
Amen.

A Prayer if Temptation Comes

Almighty God, whose blessed Son was
led by the Spirit to be tempted by Satan:
Come quickly to help us who are
assaulted by many temptations; and,
as you know the weaknesses of
each of us, let each one find you
mighty to save;
through Jesus Christ your Son our Lord,
who lives and reigns with you and
the Holy Spirit, one God, now and for ever.
Amen.

THE JESUS PRAYER

This is an ancient way of praying that involves repeating the same short prayer over and over again, out loud at first, quietly to yourself, and then, eventually, quietly inside of you.

Lord Jesus Christ, Son of God,
    have mercy on me, a sinner.

Lord Jesus Christ, Son of God,
    have mercy on me, a sinner.

Lord Jesus Christ, Son of God,
    have mercy on me, a sinner.

Lord Jesus Christ, Son of God,
    have mercy on me, a sinner.

Lord Jesus Christ, Son of God,
    have mercy on me, a sinner.

Lord Jesus Christ, Son of God,
    have mercy on me, a sinner.

Lord Jesus Christ, Son of God,
    have mercy on me, a sinner.

Lord Jesus Christ, Son of God,
    have mercy on me, a sinner.

Lord Jesus Christ, Son of God,
    have mercy on me, a sinner.

Lord Jesus Christ, Son of God,
    have mercy on me, a sinner.

JUST SIT IN GOD'S PRESENCE. ••••◦

Prayer can sometimes seem so busy. It doesn't have to be busy, and it doesn't have to involve lots of words, or any words at all. Try taking some time to simply sit in God's presence. (Don't *lie down* in God's presence—or pretend you are in bed at nighttime—because that will quickly and likely turn into *sleeping* in God's presence before long. ☺)

Roman Catholics will often sit prayerfully in God's presence in the form of the Blessed Eucharist. However you do it, in church or outside of church, know that God is powerfully all around you, listening, watching, and loving you.

Prayers while Preparing a Lenten Meal

Think about God's gifts for you and your family while you help prepare a Lenten meal of rice and beans, or bread and cheese, or spaghetti with a simple nonmeat tomato sauce . . . or whatever you happen to be eating. Even the cooking itself can be a kind of prayer.

Then, pray in a new way before you eat, maybe like this:

Bless us, O God,
and these your gifts,
that we are about to receive,
from your bounty,
through Christ our Lord.
Amen.

WHEREVER YOU ARE, REMEMBER WHAT YOU'VE MEMORIZED.

We know that there are times when you sit in church and you are bored. At those times, rather than counting ceiling tiles or annoying the people sitting near you, try sitting quietly and praying the verses of Psalm 51 that you have memorized:

Wash me thoroughly from my iniquity,
    and cleanse me from my sin.

You desire truth in the inward being;
    therefore teach me wisdom in my
    secret heart.

Create in me a clean heart, O God,
    and put a new and right spirit within me.

O Lord, open my lips,
  and my mouth will declare your praise.

Then, you can use the verses that you've committed to memory from Psalm 91 like a shield for times when you are worried or alone or just needing to talk to God. Pray them quietly to yourself. You can, after all, because you know them by heart!

My refuge and my fortress;
  my God, in whom I trust.
Under his wings you will find refuge.

He will command his angels concerning you
  to guard you in all your ways.

God says: Those who love me, I will deliver,
  and: I will be with them in trouble.

Other Stuff

BOOKS

There are other books about creative ways you can pray that you may be interested in, particularly during this time of year. Here are two:

www.paracletepress.com

Maybe you hunger to know God better. Maybe you love color.

Maybe you learn better by seeing or doing. Perhaps you can't sit still for very long, or you have a body that likes to wiggle. Prayer doesn't have to involve a lot of words. The new prayer form in *Praying in Color: Kids' Edition* can take as little or as much time as you have. Just pick up a pen, pencil, marker, or box of crayons and start to draw.

www.paracletepress.com

Maybe you like to write—did you know you can write letters to God? If you read *Writing to God: Kids' Edition* it could help you, and your parents might like to read it too. Kids see how their prayers:

Don't have to be perfect to reach God.
Don't have to use big or fancy words.
May tell a story using words or pictures.
Can be happy or sad or grumpy.
May have misspelled and crossed-out words.
  (God understands when we make mistakes.)

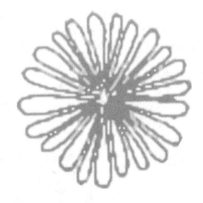

ORGANIZATIONS AND WEBSITES

Earlier in this book, we mentioned a nonprofit organization called Bread for the World. They are a collective Christian voice that urges the world's key decision-makers to do all they can to end hunger. You can check them out at www.bread.org.

Take a few minutes and google "end hunger" to read more about all the people working to help those in need.

SOURCES FOR THE PRAYERS AND PRACTICES

"Almighty God, whose blessed Son was . . ." on page 60 is from the Prayer for the First Sunday in Lent (*The Book of Common Prayer*, 1979 USA version).

The Jesus Prayer on pages 61–62 to learn more, check out the short book *Praying the Jesus Prayer: Ancient Spiritual Disciplines* by Frederica Mathewes-Green (Brewster, MA: Paraclete Press, 2011). Or the longer book *The Jesus Prayer: The Ancient Desert Prayer that Tunes the Heart to God* by Frederica Mathewes-Green (Brewster, MA: Paraclete Press, 2000.)